SOMNAMBULISM

The Poetry of James Ferace

Acknowledgments:

"The Corpse of O'Shea" - based on "The Slithery-Dee": UMFA, (C) Andrea Lagoy, (I) Jackie Lagoy, Leominster, Massachusetts, 1972, and "The Cremation of Sam McGee" by Robert W. Service.

To Edgar and Howard.

"Angustiae"

The faceless grasp
of sounds unheard
in the brush of displeasure
and ethereal pain
as we indulge
in effortless promises,
seeing with the innocence
of possession
Soul's deep in the blindness
of our names
Ashes blown from the landing
of a gentle madness
Purified fingers with remnants
of persistence
and arise in the wonder
of fertile entwining
Tasting the radiant flavor
of wasted renown
from the frigid surface,
from the disgrace of rapture
Absorbed in all conceit
towards an elegant descent

The paths of normalcy
an eternal plague on our skin
For pained is the pasture
of a wounded tongue
Nights expiring into irreverent fragments,
shining with the faces
of a hideous beauty
and hearing your sleep
in waves of eminence
In the coils of rhapsodic breaths
taken hungrily
with the fervor
of a great, vacant ocean
in nestled drops
of crystalline antipathy
The garish notwithstanding
of spiteful indulgence
A perpetual mockery,
this sentience of no pity
We, the taste
of ceaseless nonentities...

"Gallows"

Of thunder deep in fevered cool
The posthuman bane of levity
This boy undone, a blasphemous fool
who drinks the seed of longevity
Each day unled with passion's rue
A face unveiled from sanity
The sweet dissent from all of you
and absent from humanity
Embraced by your callous lips
I delved into infinity
On the cusp, my longing sips
but I've tasted my divinity
Out at the passing
The calling to weep
It's all everlasting
so now I can sleep
And now in the sounds, I talk
I breathe in severity
Unto the gallows I now walk
and see now with clarity

"Laugh of the Damned"

Though it stays with souls in shallow places
With your selfish minds and draining faces
A barren land of a thousand slaves
A sea of disease with bleeding waves
It carries along with a muted sound
Through the masses to the moistened ground
Where forgotten spirits lay to rest
in the circle sky of damp infest
On every mouth for the passing years
Upon the sweetened rain and dying fears
To infected cells in foreboding waste
To the ripened fruits of bitter taste
From a fool of time and the meek detested
of your agony song and the sad molested
You will feel the sting in your deepest core
and hear the knock on judgment's door
From the tremors of their anguish scream
The victim's sane, uncertain dream
In the quiet forest of beasts awoken
to final gasp of humanity broken
When eyes speak truth and flesh is cold
The laugh of the damned you will behold

"My Unintended"

Lamentful years beneath the mass
of rife misgiving and suffered mists
the senses of amity hymns unwritten
and I saw the plains of acts unjust

In the deepest lapse of lingering want
I dwelt not within this error of trust
but extended the gift of a core devout
and beheld not your cursory passage

Your congenial cavity twisting
the roguish juice of the glittering blessed
and in the span of charity forged
for you to expose the myth of the friend

The creation about your desire revolving
I rested my weakness upon the palms
of vengeance-minded fawns dissolving
who pillaged the germ of the familiar

The harshest gift, the dream of bliss
in the dawn of spite from Winter's anguish
to pervert the nature of loyalty
Reprisal's eye bleeds the blackest blood

Your bitter eye entranced beyond
the proudest memory of certain grace
and stole the seed to salve the burn
of those who scarred your licit face
...and slaughter the good to wound the bad.

"...and the Casualty"

So habitual, the cognizance waiting
in serpentine skin unfolding
A rational dislodge
of the inhuman misprint -
the erratum of a million irregular sentiments,
falling to fragments unyielding
In you, the lamentable trial,
who granted a favor
of limitless expense and expanse
The alluring interruption
Your infected fondness swiftly jettisons
the unfeigned adulation
and forms the chasten undertaking
The sharpest contractions
of the grievous frequency manufactures vapid
revelations,
reinventing the tribulations endlessly
The eminence of conceit
A common atrocity
The conceptual exploit
of your alleged rebirth
The greatest mockery of reason
I am left with that most blessed infringe,
which I cradle delicately
like that most acid-laced treasure,
creating the vacancy,

capturing the void
I am left evacuated,
in some kind of restless silence,
of your treasonous discomfort,
disloyal dominance
still plaguing the surface
Your loathsome scent persists
in every corner,
defying removal,
in the morning of impartial tones
Inescapable is your resigning to the palm
Requital of the torment undying
since your departure
Making a virtue of necessity, I relent
Dissolving in the serum
of your apathy
Expire to the overwhelmingly absolute
A shapeless voice,
returning to nothing

"Entropy"

Where she walked, so lies a stream
of fluid running black
And in my eyes, is there a dream
of her never coming back...
For suffering's her name
on the sour, empty moon
and the creatures never tame
on our entropy's noon
I can feel her within me
Alone she now resides
to feel the touch of he
to which evil now abides
For she was my only breath
the one that was not taken
I breathe now the passive death
from whence she shan't awaken
And in her eyes, that stream of blood
She'll taste forever soon
I drink deep the tainted flood
of our entropy's noon

"The Wasteland"

On the morn
when I tasted the angst
of the impending dusk of you
Feet sinking slowly
into your draining stare,
your ungiving eyes
In the clutch
of the frozen undying,
I partake of this river of guilt
and drink of the flowing,
inert confusion
Afflicted are the hearts
and the minds which dwell
in the mountains
of all passion
And though I swallow
your corrosive serum
of oblivion,
still I lay amongst
the jagged rocks
of your ocean
And the voices,
though they may never come,
I haunt the fields
of promise eternal
Your words are my blood,
but the lips that speak them

my bane
And again, I disintegrate
with the emptiness of touch
My element of perception,
my absurd awakening
Yet I see from my skin of remorse
you dance in the waves
of uncertainty
I can look no longer
Your sweetness of breath,
my harsh abundance
We walk the unforgiving method
of rest in a depraved empire
of toxic recollection
From the plethora of dread
From the sterile essence
...and to the wastelands
...never to awake

"Sine Qua Non"

If I could awake in her spell
from the crestfallen days
I would smile inside
for the century of ways
If I slept in her eyes
in the solitude of night
...in blindness that morn
and by day I'll have sight
She comes in glistening shades
of radiant waves, with such
anguish in me, which fades,
with the spirit of her touch
In the fortune of her glow
In the passion of our need
By the noon I will know
and every promise heed
If I could awake in her spell
from the solace of the eve
in the bliss of her name
I'll begin to believe...

"Vi"

The things I'd most like to forget
are the things I most remember
What the sadness unleashed again
on a bleak day in November
For the century worth of your tears
I can bestow these senses of youth
And with my final dying breath
I will at last tell the truth
But I am wrong once more that day
As the sun rises from within
When my paradise is in ruin
and the night terrors begin
You may know where I'll be
in that faded background inside
but feed your plants with spite
and question why they all died
They live on in spirit unwanted
That little wound you can't forget
and it bleeds with your thoughts
but dies in regret

"Somnambul"

When the night, it sings,
in severed strings
and you are caught
in coiled wings
The air is dense
with the final tense
and your words bleed,
in the mortal sense
Of the soil, which rolls,
with lasting souls
in the grounds of Heaven
with barren holes
Through the trees, it sees,
on wasted knees
with heedless ears
on suffered pleas
Memories creep
from the echoing deep
and the hands will close
to a numbing sleep
From an ache that sears
for thousands of years
From consuming guilt
to the taste of tears
To the rook, to the pawn,
to the love that is gone
in your eternal night

which knows no dawn
With the vex of the sane
in the silence of rain
The measure of calm
which was taken in vain
The smell of your hair,
the bliss of despair
into the eyes
of serenity stare
They cry with screams
of luminous dreams
and swim in light
of the mystic streams
At morn they break
when you'll awake
to the sounds of all
which with you take
The wait to endure,
the heart that is pure
but fall to the weakened
and passioned allure
Slaves we shall be
to our destiny
and bow to the hierarch,
the great fallacy

"The Grave"

When I went to the grave, my eyes did see
a friend this ground had used to be
I asked, "Oh, why, did you leave me?"
"Every day must end...and so did we."

As I seated myself on that lonely ground,
and the sullen Autumn made not a sound,
with the broken leaves that drifted around,
and my soul's great answer I had not found.

In the dreadful sand, the cursed land
My heart became too weak to stand,
and the wind, it blew, as if it knew
just how much I had yearned for you.

Yet on that calm, forsaken day
with the sky above me falling gray,
while the sticks and stones around me lay
I'd forgotten the words that you might say.

I was haunted by the sins among men,
though you beckoned me to remember when
the sun would still shine again
even if the world was all it had been.

On that fretful noon, the cursed rune,
my heart still weak in the circle moon

The wind had sorrow before tomorrow
Eclipsing the fate from which to borrow.

Still I wanted to go where you had gone
for in this mad world, I felt a pawn
and I would never stand on the placid dawn
in the skin of regret I was upon.

With the melting sun above my head,
with my hollow eyes now turning red,
the haunting thought of my burning bed,
and the empty life that I have led.

Though ever loyal, a life of toil
as I dug my hands deeper in soil
Silent you seem, perchance to dream
if the Gods of contempt would hear my
scream.

In the forming clouds, the sky is torn
and in your silence, I am born,
with that mask of smiles I have worn,
as I watch the night become the morn.

For mercy, you were deaf to my cries,
and on that grave, the winter dies,
in the subversive plain of wicked lies,
and from that ground, my soul will rise.

As I turned away on that forsaken day
I was left with nothing that I could say
In the putrid air, you were not there
My anguished heart too pained to care.

As I stood frozen at the turn
and my memories would fade and burn
on this lesson I would never learn
and for your voice, forever yearn.

For my mind you will never save
with the empty promise they have gave
like a light mist on a crashing wave
I was alone on that shallow grave.

And till this night, I have no sight
and cannot tell my wrong from right
and now I see, unpleasantly,
"Every day must end...and so did we."

"Ants in the Palm"

Rough fingers which ran
across your name
bled diligently the disregard
as I was born pallid
and unremitting.
Legs crossed over
drizzling narcoleptic tongues,
the severed tolerance
of the shattered and eager
You wear the soft,
pink razorwire face
of exposed nerves within
your fractured stability,
spitting debased elements
of withheld compost and bone
Scratched internally by the jagged,
prophetic teeth,
the rotting gathering of nail and rib
which pull and bargain with all my
extraneous,
pale endings
The wasting mind
of those just below
where I sat amongst
the blessed scourge

wherein the breach
of my flesh is persecuted
Sat and fondled
the solvent blister of we,
the preborn and tampered with
Left omnipresent
and licking the growth
of all foreshadowing fluids
soaking through
my scar tissue patchwork
The rough and splintered fingers
which ran across
your explicit name,
but dwindling voice,
persist in wrapping
the fabric tighter
- squeezing and wrenching,
singing the choking reverb
in the collagen puddles
The merciless peeling
of whorish valiance
curling and dropping like wax
on the machination scrotum,
gnawing through
the organic bondage
only to reveal
the steel beneath
Drawn and wrung from
the exhausted seedling
of leprous answers

and slivered corneas
in all capsized permanence
Peace in violation
Beauty in the abscessed
Quenched in sulfuric trickles
from concrete monikers
and disabled obedience
The ceaseless flow
of sour abundance spilling
onto the incisions
of stinging moments
and menstruating cavities
Where degenerates feed,
where the needles need -
disjointed and twisted fingers
once ran across
your absent name,
your echoed voice
from ages gone,
the clotting dust drifting
from my empty fist
and the deflowering cyst,
creating dunes
of inhibition and animus,
seeping through the cotton
and staining it
with castrated breath.
Within the throes,
which never will know bounds,
the corrosive remedy

"Grain de Sel"

A thousand storms
of gentle misery
became a paradise
of the infamous mist
Pleasantly degraded in ages
of proverbial spite,
feel the grasp loosen
The flawless abrasion lays
in sound awareness,
removed precisely
from solemnity,
from the malice
of distance,
the cruelty
of surroundings
and of birth
You're to blame
The burning hand
of the wounded visage
continues to envelope
the viral dependence you wipe
from your face
in the meticulous denial,
with magnificent patterns crumbling
into needless will

I breathe in with careless complacency
of each bitter moon transuding
sympathetic liquors
of illiterate failure
A wasted tribulation
With your guilty hands
In your weak, pathetic little soul -
the forged blessing
of cures without infection,
the concrete growth
inside unnurtured debauchery
The discharge of self-preservation
I am never to awake
in the mouth of lunacy
The comforting strain
Loathsome and everlasting,
they penetrate obstructed ears
and thrust deep,
feeling the pinch of dissolve
You're to blame
Breached solace
The urgency of relief
Sleeping in the midst
of each peeled layer,
basking in subversive seclusion,
the beloved lateral bruise
weeping ambrosial distortion -
proving infinitum what comes forth
from this tortured loss
is little more than mist...

"Embolus"

To lay within malignant hand
and give to thee this heart of sand
Upon the fray of fraudulent bliss
A burden of a dismal kiss

Amidst the pang of suffering hidden
The marred union with joy forbidden
Muted silence where passions melt
The voiceless breed with vengeance dealt

Indignant soil of a wordless birth
Synthetic nature and freakish worth
Resentment fills a sutured soul
This rendered chance in redeemer's role

Pleasant fatigue of a liquid fold
Toothless words of secrets told
The rotting beast which falls to waste
A faceless pawn to be replaced

This choking dream of a wilting grace
Nullified love in a liar's embrace
Gifts of content to seduce and entice
The euphoric wing...aborted precise

"Bones of Contention"

As each century is kissed
with Machiavellian lips
in the cathartic drought of sentiment,
we pass elusively beyond askew deduction
and lay dying in the listless oasis
of our withering subconscious
Within the bondage
of every tumultuous inception,
we still ride atop the horses of mockery,
never questioning
when we will let them drink
The oceans of fortune will forever
remain the antagonists
of the cerebral's greatest inspiration
And though I beg to partake
of your fervent flesh,
with honest distress and veracious
disobedience
to the multitude's apropos,
you will always bathe
in the puddles of ridicule,
leaving me thirsting for the fluids
of genesis emanated
Truly it is us who are plagued
in the shadow

of convulsion's dignity
And the years will pass
with I still waiting
in the gardens of scorn,
reading intently
from the pages of retribution...
and memorizing their sounds,
listening closely
for all their entozoan voices,
which brush against
my exposed strain
Strain pensively to dwell within you,
if for a spell
Receiving their message clearly
that sparse are the pure
and damned
are they who do rest
in the eon
of the rampant avaricious
Defaced is all
which should be embraced
amongst the harsh tempest
We are silence

You are there
I am nowhere
We are epidemic
It claws and pulses
with every absorption
and I willfully drink it down

with unfavorable penetration
For every trespass enacted
upon chaste grass,
the illicit malefactor
of the shameless
Still I desire
...with empty virtues
and dirty fingers wanting to touch,
regardless of their mire
For the one I see before me
is the antithesis
of all that I was
and all that I could never be
And I see your face through all
of this chaotic displacement,
in the chasm of plenty yet of none,
you are the mouth of resistance
in my kindred
of shattered prophecies.
Still the syringe which carries
the saturnine fracture
of the communal purpose
will to this day remain broken
by the dearth of sound
And when I try to repair this,
I only cause myself to bleed further
And bleed I do, as do we all,
in our own enraptured bleakness.
Each morning we breathe
in the company of ourselves,

unable to comprehend
the willingness
of the soil's determination
to see what we ignore,
to cure what we have defiled,
to awake the ignorant,
and destroy the dullards
But we shall never perceive
our own hatred,
which seeps from our hands
in the precision of extravagance,
the path of which we succumb
...and march we will through the door of
trepidity now

"Err"

There is no release
I see a dearth in the eyes
of all the unappetizing
little wretches,
with every sword you swallow,
knowing my secreting voice
The social acceptance
and the passions
of my chainsaw memories
Literal thoughts and the color
of ink become impure
when that beast
comes from its cave
Tongue slides gracefully
and wantingly
across your aluminum friction,
submitting fully
to the ejaculate undertow
The serpentine gush
of dancing plasma washes over us,
I tear at the thread
which keeps my lids prisoner
from the release of sight
Upon their breaking,
I feel it all peel away,

the taste of peach absent
from my grasp,
and the pitiless pinch
of sterility rebounds
Thumbs severed
Still dead in your imagined lap,
where there is no peace
No calm
No tension
No push
No release

"Victual"

You have drank of the Heavens above us
You have hidden away in your sleep
You have tasted the soul that I give you
in the precious oasis you keep
I would bleed to be in your pasture
I have screamed the sorrow I reap
But my cries of pain are all silenced
in the precious oasis you keep
In your heart I am a prisoner
to your eyes I have fallen in deep
Yet today, alas, I am starving
for the precious oasis you keep
Will your ears ever awaken?
Into them my words ever seep?
Am I again to ever be welcomed
in the precious oasis you keep?
So now I lay here dying
and my flesh will gently weep
at the sight of you all alone
in that precious oasis you keep

"Hibernal Ardor"

Deliver me, please,
from smoldering ashes
from stitching undone,
the cruelest purge
The distress of dawn
with days impaled
Slowly wasting to
the dust of my reason
An aching sedative
of anemic disquiet
Your unsound cure
defiles the water
The malignant swallow
consecrating the image
of torturous devotion,
maltreated hands
Skinning and plaguing
a virtuous affection
Abrasions surfacing
in the grief of doubt
To the burial of
this fleeting Avalon
of questionable sincerity,
the ceaseless loyalty uncertain
I accept this torment,

regretless of sense and sensation
Beyond trepidation that it is
the proof of existence
Evermore lamenting
the desolate consequence
Lay we in ruins
of shattered elements
to the cremation
of this righteous adulation
in the resting place of assurance
For with boundless fortitude
will I mourn you

"A Coercion"

Now horizons clear
with colors defined
in the obscure committal
of introspection
I taste the order of mortality
and sit in the glow
of complacency, once
And I may soon again drink
of your unequivocal sacrifice,
which has given me
a new name
Though I abide
with burrowing grace
and egocentric truth,
the hearing of will sustains
when the whole legion emerges
in the trust of the guilty
And we will be
Decrepit limbs
and punctured eyes
will still behold
the hollow of the dominant unity
The element of disorder,
the encircling of the misshapen
Soon we will pray

at the altar of rationale
The callous will become
the things of legend
and the sullen will fade
with the inequities of season
We will tread
the roads of recognition
and become lost regardless,
always possessing
erudition of little pith
But the snows
of triviality will fall
on barren proverbial tables
and the hungry shall here
and forever altercate
while the submissive
revolve and purge
Though we swallow
the seeds of manipulation
and though I still dehydrate
from my thirst of midnight,
I sense with your skin
and I speak with your tongue
the verses of enslavement's end

"Flesh Pendulum, I"

Within your divine walls
I melt for a spell of sacred rapture
Ethereal shapes below me
that encase my starving structure
in your seraphic embrace
In agony for the little death
I confront in your name
I am born within you

"Fathom"

Blind to your ways
I follow, unquestioned
to the march of the narrow
The empty, the sad, the hungry for
knowledge
Farewell to your Hell, fall in line
and speak the words you are fed
Taste not of the flesh,
worry not, I will still embrace you
Drink deep the stories of old
Turn your back
on the sullen forgotten, evil
Find your own way and suffer
Drink not and die in
the shallow pool
without ever having lived

"Viscera"

Push me off the dust
of your narcotic fringe,
never partaking
of a forgiving eon,
where needs go to die
Only of relics
The blessing of your flesh
more than I
in this centurion catastrophe
called being
Every foot that hits the ground
in the name of lust
draws back a frame
of toes broken and shamed,
cracked and leaking
the latex immunity
Techno-colored carnal refund
Genital rebate
The acid burn of hope
Testicular emancipation.
That elephant graveyard
of skin and sweat,
long since withered and dried
A world of lambs
and leopards
of the castrated sort

The becoming.
The sad little pull
in the ethical salutation
The angel covered
and covering
in creational fluid remains an angel,
still searching
for the valley
in which night seamlessly
bleeds with day
Simultaneous defense
and repellence
of the perverse
The capsized vessel where
the pillars shall meet
and lay in the great,
sung gale of the forgotten pulse
This frigid,
hollow dwelling I lay,
still begging
for your sacred acceptance

"Abilene"

In all my days, I had never seen
A face like that of my Abilene
A face that would become my cure
From a girl like a river pure
In her eyes, I would heal
In my eyes, she was real
Though to you, a richer dream
She always is as she may seem
Through the mountains of silent sleep
She is buried in memories deep
I behold life on her skin fair
In her arms, I am without care
And still I kept each word she'd say
when our blue skies turned to gray
Yet once she grew blind to need
She closed her eyes to watch me bleed
Still she hung in the empty sky
She opened her eyes to hear me die
...and in my last of days I'd still never seen
A face like that of my Abilene

"L'enfant Terrible"

In this skin lies agitated psalms chanting
from sumptuous machines which grind
to the resplendent tones of dementia's strings
The salacious creation laments
as it forges designs
of perpetual craving, and slips;
down, down through ornamental falls
and the profanely narrow,
where I taste the faint echoes
of a puerile haze
From a time when I drank
from its abundance,
and all that is paralyzed becomes animated
amongst a septic mist,
but is distilled once more in the light
of your vacant musings
And I feel reverberations of choirs
of voices singing false praises
of the sickeningly pedestrian

"Solus"

In desolation comes the creation of will
In isolation I will remember you still
But I fold the desperate hour with me
And so shall you remain - a memory

"Of Gods and Roaches"

Once upon a splintered soul
an element of torment
in a cursed, vile, forsaken hole
lies a being laying dormant

In the fading of the Autumn glow
the hollow, purple sky
is a place that few will know
and no one wonders why

Within the quiet, chilly vent
we hear the breath of regret
The sullen cries were never sent
and their needs always unmet

And the Winter never showed its face
for the creature greatly feared
Many were wise to leave this place
and those they told adhered

An entity to be ignored
Those who fled its tongue
for the lost it cleaved and gored
and feasted on their young

Not a word they longer speak
in myths did they all revel
They just turned their other cheek
and blamed it on the Devil

And time finally came
when all began to doubt
and there was no one to blame
when it decided to come out

Still they sat upon their knees
in all their grand chagrin
Hands clasped in the freeze
of the insects on their skin

They could close their eyes no more
and the myth was now dispelled
as they bled, it was known
that the evil shan't be held

And on that day when streets ran red
in the service of pain it broaches
Only in the reign of the dead
will we see of Gods and roaches

"Father"

How is it that I sensed your dying descent
when you sat across from me in May?
In the coming June, you paused when the
cruelty of passage stunted your breath
I breathed for you, but could not stop
the pain that surged and stung
in the halls where complacency hung
Heavy came the words in July
Seven years unto a Sunday morning
when my compassion was erased
and my raped heart replaced
with the diseased rivers of loneliness
I missed the words you would say to me
I had so much more to learn from you
What you gave me indispensible
It is all I have left
My fortunes all for one last day
where those words just would not come
But why could I not even cry?
You were a better man I
and I never got to say goodbye...

.

"Votre Nom"

With untreated wounds,
I asked calmly their desires
So said they a name familiar,
was I left fingerless on this noon
which was vanquished
in the treasury of a moment
So said they,
this word which would bestow upon me
a deafness so welcomed
in knowing my ear's eternal blessing of it,
this title I would be within the presence of,
on that echoing death of sound
Though I'd begged them for silence
in nights of denial,
for the fruitless cravings,
undying thirsts unquenched
So said these elements, regardless,
like the dripping wax of the relentless
and the beads of moisture
unreaching the arid
No matter the volumes of screams,
they could not drown all which dwells
in the realms of the evident
So here I lay,
unsung in the missions of stifled blame,

with no eyes to see,
but a voice to speak,
with which I asked calmly their desires
So said a name eulogized
by my abundant void
Elevated by this celestial entity,
though afflicted by fierce distance,
I lapse into the remorse of memory,
the ministry of delusion,
my only liberation
On such scarlet evenings,
I ask calmly once more these longings
which bask in my unyielding lesions
...and so said they your name

"Laetitia"

Find me not upon
the branches of lustful falls,
yet amongst the celestial children gone
in the black sleep of misting fountains
Akin to pallid creatures, I walk,
with grasped gatherings of shattered wings
and ethereal tears -
to fill the ocean of judgement renowned
I think not of residence bleeding,
but of providence pleading
in those infertile lands of shining apathy
with passionate tides that now be still
Still within the beloved song
of the eyes of twilight
For I am washed in the shade of paling jade,
which stands against the ritual of time
Alas, the forgotten serene waters
which stir beneath us in the aftermath of
devoted unrest - manifest
They manifest,
be us in the motionless silence
of the witching clouds that weep
in distances above
Yet you wear the valentine veil
of torn empires in the labyrinth of angels

I wear not the unholy belief
of transmissive sunshine
I am but the melting dream of infancy
The drifting mythical spirit
of patriarchal reason
Entombed in the blanket of the dawn,
where eternal birth and immortal earth
come looking down with the threshold
of the cursed unknown
When I rest upon my laurels
and my good graces

"The Ecstasy of the Broken Skin"

In the treasured element
within every breath of infancy
The reverie, the spectres
of fortune that smile
at the winds of the displaced and amidst
For I loved beyond sempiternity...
and limit not within
the eternal ways with my vision
of a defeated mystery
Still I returned home to a forest
of distant awakenings...
and I waste away in your
morose nights, holding hands with infinity,
haunted by my own name
I've braved the horizons
of a blurred memory
within this mortal dream
When the morning rises
and tears of rain descend abruptly
You slept quietly in the hatred
of all that we were
I began to witness reflections
of the afflicted within me,
in the river of my answers
Such delicious grief

and gorgeous lacerations
you left me with
Though I have fallen passed
every spiteful word
and passive needles thrown
With tired feet and tired eyes,
I walk away with soul undefiled
Licking the exudes
from drizzling apologies
On the cusp of images,
walking aside you on wintry days
Eternity removed
from time and with tide
The jagged rocks of your foolish ocean,
your oblivion
I partake...and drink of the flowing guilt,
the inert confusion
At the expense of a fractured spirit
and fatuous sense
for impaired are the hearts and minds
which dwell in the mountains of all passion
and down we lay our heads in regret

"Consacré"

You are the most indulgent fate
The plight of fortune's chance
and beyond the torturous wait
We'll fulfill the spirit's dance
The delicious bond we share
is the covenant unto me
Yet, perhaps, it is not there
in this true totality
My life, my air, the blood in my veins
You become every purpose
The blanket when it rains
and plunge deeper than the surface
I am aware and I mourn
for every second missed
and without my angel born
Will yearn not to exist
To be the name upon your tongue
The deepest pore beneath your skin
and the final aria sung
I'll end where you begin
And when our flesh is one
You will hear me in your voice
Our union shall be done
If you only had a choice
This night of mortal fusion

Your precious element
and your crystalline illusion
of your cursed fatigue sent
And though alone you'll grieve
in scorned solidity
I will make you believe
and you will become me

"Immortal Wretch"

So little mean
the ones who consume
and buried in all
their intentions
The removed spine
to taste of the missing
In the balance
of invaluable pity
A pathetic ghost,
a demise is your worth
Feed off the afflicted,
praise those underneath
Cognitive perversion,
a life truncated
Supernal necrophilia,
a blessing sans sympathy...
The pulse
of the sickeningly uninteresting
with an observation
of the blind
An audible syringe
on your spiritual shelf
Passing a release,
not a detriment
You bled the saints dry

to drink
the orgasmic bile in grief -
Sweet grief
The performance
will become the sliver
This is ours now yours,
this prayer
of miniscule comfort

"Mourning, Tedium"

The miserable apology to all infected
Tears of the eyeless savior
Severed nerves of the suffered eternal
On mirthful days with edgeless reason
to pierce the lens of the shattered
and it all lays twitching, withering in fatigue
A brooding place, a lifeless face
The rife hand circulates the pallid green
Horizons unbound are certainly seen
Those hungry for the pitiful eye
Hoping for someone close to die
and I'm bathed in the nauseating tone
of those in the vein of the limbless lustful
Those pathetic creatures, say I...

"Fatum"

In love, we live
with the radiant call
In life, we give
though in death, we fall
A breath, a plight
of transient dreams
Of day, of night
in cultured streams
Our birth, a curse
a blessing or gift
For better, for worse
we straddle the rift
The divine error
the incredible fault
We are the barer
in the Earth of salt
We bleed, we burn
to be in the light
You bruise, you learn
in eternal night
With scars, we grow
passed all the absurd
With what we sow
then turn all inward
Through years, we prove

we breed then kill
So desperate to move
but only stand still
The sound, the guilt
the essence of snow
The bridge we built
can never let go
A place, a taste
a chill of resent
Deface, the waste
of sour repent
In sorrow, in gray
we will rise to be
The shelter, the way
to drown destiny

"Agon et Dormis"

Deep in pestilence, he guided
with placid thoughts unseen
and touched gracefully
the fervid senses held in secrecy
Her hand, moistened,
glides adversely with desperate words
and sights of guile,
feet rough on broken fences -
and slips
A merciless rest of sainted ire,
beyond his will of the fateless design,
the prophet restrained
in a motionless storm
The call of the sea finds her uncovering,
toiling,
in the divisive empire
of her insatiable essence
Legs evolving into tangled structures
folded amongst the corralled tempest...
though her transporting light diffuses
and satiates each ember,
quenching seared replicas of sentiment
An unfettered shelter nestled
in turbulent dementia,
overlooking elevations of old,

where travelers concede the sufferer's wake -
all for an instant of the divinity she speaks
Still, apparitions hold him
in a fool's obedience
while the noxious entities on the far side
of elaborate inception
are calling to the ghosts
of covetous disquiet
Deep in indulgence, he guided
with detached constancy ignored
and seized morosely
the distorted succession
fractured by uncertainty
Her hand, chafed, closes unfilled
with prosaic tones and etches of the arcane,
feet hardened to glorious stone
...and sleeps

"Terminus"

She pierces delicately,
with harmless respite
With that most gentle pretense
- a timid soul
of synthetic interior
and a breath of the naive
The consummate familiar
- a brilliant facade
The new dawn rising
breeds abhorrent modes
which reveals designs
of elegant insecurities
Birthing all my nightmares
into fruition
with merciless hunger
and heedless inhumanity molds
and continues feeding them to the day
with equal sums
of ignorance and malice
Dissecting tolerance,
pleasantries absolved
and abandons such benign semblance behind
in the wake of the dead
The fingers of charity,
cancerous and rotting

To satiate the ever-growing
cravings of she
Whom will never know contentment -
and suffer those near
Cleansing herself of the mire
of the sincere
In her delusion of resurrection
Beyond disregarded genocide
- she is reborn
Until the succession resurfaces...
and commences once again...

"In the Offing"

In the offing where bearings fade
with wings of glass and tears of jade
The clarity of one breath's embrace
in a tranquil skin of apathy's face
Dissolving with touch, a sullen amiss
Exposing the light of a wordless bliss
Eyes of stone drip beads of dust
and faithless shards will sleep to rust
Of poisoned wells to drink and swallow
A sutured road you blindly follow
Unproven rapture on shallow ground
Where every move defiles the sound
and bonds diminish in an adequate term
and sacred to thee, an elegant germ
A covetous rogue in persona hidden
Will forlorn and the plague beridden
A sin of the barren upon the coil
In the offing, where none are loyal

"Sagacity"

Anointed, but not my friend
Although I was told otherwise,
and I believed
To the east I found
my betrayer
Whom I gave my blood to
Only to be judged
But you had no right
As I found the evil in me
throughout the years
You idly watched over
my tormentors
My molesters you gave life to
So some say
I now remove myself
from your false prophetic reign
You've stopped living,
stopped breathing in my view
But my goodbyes, like my pleas,
fall on deaf ears
I'd tear out your heart if you had one
A life, a soul, a person to a myth devout
These very words a void
Now it is I, not you,
who will manifest

And fall and cry and live and die
Though death is too easy
You escaped without disturb
Where I lost you without sorrow
And I find my strength in your absence
Should you make yourself known again
It won't take a horde
I shall crucify you myself
...and rewrite the fable

"Sleep of Evensong"

Transmissive days
with concrete tears
A gravel haze
as evening nears
The lullaby straits
of a million miles
A warning waits
showing melting smiles

Mating spasms
in your fallout bend
Progress chasms
of your timeless end
Greed of the land
and obsolete thunder
The ignorant hand
of one nation under

Aborted hope
with denial stain
A fraying rope
as the voices drain
Sugar coated mesh
of demons faced
And the bloated flesh
of the aftertaste

This immigrant blue
in the sleepless age
And welcome to
the ashen rage
Angels of rape
in the depraved lust
The longing escape
and we all die must

A platinum skin
with the blade nearby
A suicide grin
we have heard on high
On the shore they glisten
with the stories said
In the night they'll listen
to the song of the dead

With the traveler's ghost
in a child's bed
On the golden coast
with the ocean's dead
From the father's grief
to the mother's dread
To the lost belief
of the voice of the dead

To the thought
which lingers in the Devil's head
And is wrought
into calliope's dead
In the books of arcane
the keeper read
And the doomed insane
in the fields of the dead

Where the rivers flow
in the colors of red
And the weeds that grow
where others fled
This place mankind
does fear to tread
and be unkind
to the hangman's dead

"Inamorata"

In harmonious grasps
where anguish is neutral
Moving elsewhere
from covering mischance
In the coma
of your selfish portraits
so many leprous shavings
in exchange for muzzles
Seedlings of insignia,
the gesture within naked hands
and drowned mouths
breeding new skin
The deafening mute
in an ocean of smiles
This tyrannical face,
uttering infections
and singing penetration
for the disappointment
of the blistering profane
of the coils
in your unheard mediocrity song
Watch you burn
with choking retinas

and purely unhinged grief
Purging the tainted
in a self-fulfilled prophecy
of synthetic abandon
as a dog to its vomit...
I swallowed your desperate breath
with little resistance
and barely recalled
your tedium, floating...
to the surface of your puddle
Nurtured by the milk
of the tick in the wound
The leech on the muted pore
Perverts and saints
All become one
in an underline of calm
and you're no longer welcome here...

"The Year of the Rat"

Blistering dimly, the insect's tongue
the scourge ingests the fallible weakness
in fluent sweeps of bacterial growth
this fraudulent animal of silence avowed
from the bowels of chance
in the guise of a siren
Granting the swine safe passage
to the recesses of your sediment
The abomination
is your contaminated discourse
She disfigures everything she touches
A vermin's womb in seraph's dress
Conjuring only the dissolute
which spreads apart and squanders
the very dust upon your essentia
Scream as you may this empty incant
Your adored creation would disgorge you
and you'll await misfortune
with lips sewn tightly

"Dyad"

Shown you pain in outlines clouded
Cherish the smite of animus shrouded
In purity's gaze when moons advance
In false admire Chimera's trance

Dead eyes blink with blank serene
In every cell which won't die clean
Dissolving faith of a colorless trust
Umbratic wraith which turns to dust

On begging knees where reckons fall
Transparent pleas of a stifled call
Planting the neglect of mistaken seeds
...and break you not of no one's needs

Fallen asunder on knees abruise
A victim of your greatest ruse
With lips ashorn to beg the names
With tongue in palm of sickened games

A night of days can never see
The sum of nothing can never be
Taste the hollow between you and I
...and let this miserable child die

"Terra di Merda"

I see the dawn again in patience
though I never gave it ground
I was younger in my lesions
and I still await the hunger
I became what I most ignored
and all I was is now drawn
Peel it off to look inside again
though all I see are spoils
The depth of this expansion
is the hemorrhage of form
and the growth becomes consuming
While the juices eat the cure
so your eyes return benign
In the rust of this corruption
is the face of weeping cold
When the ghosts of discontentment
bring you gifts of broken sores
Tell the dream it is time I awake
Beg the spirit to now be whole
Feel the flesh upon the conscience
Bridge the void beneath the spine
Though the teeth may scratch and puncture
I can still admire how pure
my hands remain in bondage
Yet my tongue may see the distance
Still, only graves know intention

For the ink will stain your fingers
That's as far as they will run
From the twisting worm of substance
In an age of no diversion
When the ghosts of discontentment
bring you gifts of broken sores

"Coil"

One, oh, sweet one
how you disappoint me so
From my eyes, a crimson rain
stains the newly-fallen snow
But your eyes, oh, your eyes
how they beckoned me to come
Fingers bleed to touch you
yet you left me feeling numb
On that crisp Autumn eve
how I ran to your voice
When it entered my conscience
and took away my choice
"Finally", thought I, "now it will awaken...
...and be worth all of the pain."
Though, perhaps, I was mistaken
Came out from the shadows
and, alas, the price I paid
though I basked within your glow
...perhaps I should have stayed
Found a hole, crawled inside
and breathed a solemn breath
Tossed it on the wheel of chance
and died a lonely death
Found a scab, began to pick
"How did I get so low?"
One, oh, sweet one
How you disappoint me so

"Nadir"

My winter in claustrophobic wombs
The hiatus passing severs the cord
and drips restraint from weary figures
Narcoleptic fragments give way
with dwindling features
gone astray

Terrified of season's decline
Splintering from notions surging
Capable of far worse things
Though blameless is petrified
Interfere and temper's gone
Behind the curtain the beast is drawn

To give it passage
and the chains will fall
Possessing the reverence
though they inherit the ruins

Lapsing through the spoils,
in perpetual faint
Fathomless cores with untold pitch
Regarding the obstructed
with unforeseen empathy
with infantine anguish
and fetal calm

The averse undertaking throughout
confined neurosis crawling
regretting the coarse rapture
disabling the lucid
idling amidst the arcane
Pretending the burden will wane

"Septic Baptism"

When divine aches smother
in the blister of night
Your catalyst of fables
and whispers despite
My absence divides
with death on your skin
the elixir of venom
your swallow of sin
When your name he breathes
The seedling of scorn
He'll choke on the plague
of pureness well worn
The essence of whores
on the heels of neglect
The faceless impure
your greatest defect
To sever the tongue
A germ of conceits
So blind, the cunt
The cycle repeats

Though alive within your arms
touched death across your skin
beneath your gaze
the pang's breeding
and my hand closes, empty
for the agonizing moment

until you are amidst once more
within my starving grasp
with angelic eyes and sacred rest
to fill the vacant adore
I glimpse demise in your abandon
and arise once more in your vision

"Meridian"

The wisdom of my yesterday lays me down
and talks long of greener fields...
still I smile at the collapse of tomorrow,
as each scratched bruise gives me life
and bleeding ears fill your fountain of lies
I ascend the hill of sanctity
alone and puzzled,
handed words I need not hold nor want.
Take the knife and press it to your throat,
wash your filthy hands
in the many rules of contention
Pave your road with the cement of bitterness
and walk until your toes splinter

"The Taste of Antipathy"

Upon this blank canvas,
my hand will be gone and replaced
with a vengeful mind
The paint of the roses will drip off
the surface of hope
Gaze at the sleeping beast
with reckless detachment
as your scars wither and fade
Bring me the open pastures
of my gray eyes and the missing sky
I see how far we've come
Those distant places,
all dressed in faces of whimsy and deceit
Come run with me,
away to the castles of the displaced
and clouds of the erased
For I loved you with a love
that was beyond the seas
Still I returned home to a forest
of infected offerings...
and I wasted away in your castrated grin
I've braved the horizons
of a blurred memory within
this mortal dream
I took your pain and possessed its children,
to which you became blind
But I saw. And I still see...how far we've come

How we have gotten nowhere
You slept quietly in the absence
of all that we were,
as you will once more
I awoke once again in the aftermath of vision
On the cusp of never, you'll awake
and I will feel without apology
For I loved you with a love
that was beyond the seas
Though in my sane senses will I let you go

"The Boy Who Could Not Die"

There once was a boy
who could not die
and his tongue was a tongue
that could not lie
For a lie is a word
that can bring only pain
So he spoke only truth
to those he had slain

When the dead returned
to avenge their souls
He had dug his garden
full of holes
One-by-one,
he buried them again
and he was crowned
a king among men

As years went by,
the boy did not age
He continued to kill
to suppress his rage
He buried his mother
on the backfield hill
and he held a banquet
to toast each kill

At night he'd awake
to the voice of a ghost
and decided to leave
his home on the coast
But wherever he went,
he was not alone
to pay the price
of flesh and of bone

Again and again,
the question he'd keep
What he wouldn't give
to finally sleep
They tapped on glass
and pounded on walls
and shouted his name
down the hallowed halls

Decades pass
and still came no rest
and tears filled up
his lonely nest
Tossed and he turned,
that boy would cry
"What I would not give
to finally die!"

"Filius Populi"

The aptness of your pride,
your grandest virtue
Yet, in the atrophy
of belief lays your contempt
Crossbred fool,
in glory there is waste
under the guise
of the oppressed,
you strain
Slaving to sire
the ingenuine masquerade
But you bleed hollow dissent
and the mire
of your vanity
does not nurture all
Trust as you may
in the volumes
though you are buried
The resources befall your intentions
with the conceit
of your apparent surface
The mortal swelling
is the miscarriage of a man
Your dispensable flair,
your barren utterance
The personal gravity you contain
A singular current

to which none reside
For sullen appeal,
a fashion accessory
Your influence minimal
in this certain extent
The mass of fatigue
with your vaunting dignity
to be blessed
to live in your world
Crossbred fool,
in glory there is waste

"Torso"

In the removed absorption
of your tender fringe
where grievous intent slides
across longing expanse
yearning to sever
stained strings running
slick with misgivings
and beautiful contempt
with depthless stigmas
molding the vast facade
the defected cavity animated
the mesmeric frame
imbued in the womb
of soulless infirmity
Unfolding in warm
afflictions stinging
in agreeable motions
for tender shame,
for the intolerable
and the urbane
I will diverge
in aberrant shapes
disfigured always
misborn endlessly, swimming
in the impure prime
unfathered and affable
All poorly encumbered

in the mortal forenoon
I remain weak,
inert to indisposed equity
of anemic discharge,
interminably flowing moist
into the frailest hands
obscured in pallid corners

"Flesh Pendulum, II"

Smother me in sweltering tissues
and the severity of your altitude
For the ground that shifts
in my intimate agony,
I wait in this wicked cloak of days
Fill my glass and allow me
to sate my undying coitus thirst,
Me, a slave of your growing soil
This pleasant debauchery,
your exquisite quicksand,
habitual mental suicide
I am eternally awakened by invasion
and, upon bloody knees,
beg to taste your radiant flavor
Face embracing rawness
with such careless abandon
Heaven and earth transcending
the wonderful torment you serve to me
The tolerated ache,
a chronic disturbance in an angel's veil
My tongue held captive,
engulfed in this paradoxical cell
My sickest hungers, I crucify
I trespass on the tortured pink and perspire
on this somatic threshold
A falling spectacle of carnal breath isolated
in a moist casualty

Long, yes, to have dwelt
in the shadow of perversion,
the sinister urge
We become beautifully unclean
Your sensual plague upon my skin
with my release,
though I die over your lips
in the cherished cravings unquestioned
Within your divine walls,
I melt for a spell of sacred rapture
Ethereal semblances below me
which encase my starving structure,
your seraphic enfold
My substance remedied by the sweet
appetence
of your muliebral elixir
Anguish fades with the little death
we have confronted in the other's name

"Elegiac"

Of the flawless and eternal
and illusory being
Stirring figments of tangible,
spectral sounds
in the trueborn deluge
of mythic discord
The harmonic dream
of the tuneless call
All we conceive,
the grotesque veracity
Binding the virtuous eye
of sweet erosion
Summoning the eminence
of such marvelous ridicule
In nights of demented revenants
and speculations
Illustrious fragments raining
in heinous confessions
The aberrant cell splitting
and perverting simple dignity

"The Strychnine Serenade"

Beyond the hills lies a solitary man,
the most desolate creature in all of the land
He stands alone on the grassy slopes,
full of misery, but somehow copes
Until now, he sat, that most pitiful man,
swallowing the pills he's poured in his hand
They go right down with a gulp and lick
They shred his insides and make him sick
He bleeds from the mouth, nose, and the ear
Screams and he screams, but no one will hear
His hair, it sheds, his skin, it peels
and no one for miles cares just how he feels
His eyes, they burst, his lips, they split,
skin turns to dust, his heart turns to shit
Fingers snap off and fall to the soil,
insides loosen and begin to uncoil
Just at this moment, with his bloody eyes,
he sees with good sense that he never will rise
beyond where he stands with his scarred soul,
so he drops to his knees,
Earth swallows him whole
and lays in his place of rest all alone,
to cry in a place where flesh becomes bone
His poisoned mind sinks in even deeper
With his swollen tongue,
he laughs at his keeper
A cold gust blows, stealing his last thread

He lays there alive, yet he lays there dead
This once good soul just melts in distress
He started with little and ended with less
This pile of ash that once here laid
is replaced by the sounds of the strychnine
serenade...

"Dreams of Malice and Blithe"

Bane is the man removed from creation
Amiss is the soul, the victim
of thoughtless penetration
Those evil little moments
I am the savior
and the purveyor of nothing
Fingers bleed from the ghosts which drag me
Perhaps we'll meet again
in the clouds of contempt
That sick, tired day of depravity
Still I wonder why the Earth perishes
beneath my disgusted feet
Do not save me this time,
when I praise inside the distance
and suck deep the weakness -
your odium
I peel back the corruptive skin
in a blank, unending shiver
But passed all the fallen shackles,
souls wait patiently for a plateau
of distancing misfits
Engulfing the nonsense,
embracing all that is broken and torn -
lick the sulfur from ashen debris
When the past is a friend
and the future an enemy
To a victim, trust wanders aimlessly,

but never rests in sovereign beds
The gloriously fucked
I will always rise in the passive dement
as I feel the mire
of your wound spill upon me
I am the accepting degenerate once more
I make friends
with the spirits there
Consequence is of the divine fallen children
in this exquisite realm
of the muted undying
Passing grief for what the hermit sees
For every rising plain once called eternity
within the saddened woods
where passions roam
Shining then fading in all closed eyes
Brilliant shadows which crawl and slither,
leaving trails of guilt and the moist,
adored complexity of duration
Overlooked by all,
yet this bastard soul absorbs the whole
...and corrodes unsung

"Sacrificial Lamb"

When the child shifts and awakes
in empty wombs and lethargy lakes
We swim inside those platinum cores
of sparkling suns and bleeding sores
To lick the wounds of weeping days
and still I felt your passioned gaze
of whence the neon flesh will peel
in the shadow of ruin, I will feel
To die in your name is just the same
as living when the insects came
and twitch when they begin to crawl
Repent as the immortal fall
Listen as they pant and scream
and fold within your plastic dream
The sleep of cold, metallic trances
In your embrace, a demon dances
in the hearts of those of broken bane
and those who drink the sweetest pain
What you give in the name of scorn
and your touch a bitter thorn
That suicide kiss you forever send
When light is a foe and darkness, my friend

"Prolix"

As I knelt down into the damp passing
When the grasp of infamy reached out to me
Driven down, finding me still
a questionable presence
I witness the calculated injustices
with which all previous days fell with you
With great persistence,
cowardice in the face
of my destructive fingers
Even to the isolation of others
with subversive anger entering
From the tall fields where I have walked
in the overpowering wind of contemplation
I have bitten through my tongue
and can taste
the sour solution of my bastardized reason
with no cure for the masked judgment
My kind hand eaten by your complacency
and I drink it down in the face of a twisted,
safe mirage which was never to be
and I am left with
my cancerous introspection
in my fallen embryo of hate undying...

"Animus"

I see you holding hands with confusion,
your hair nestled around your chin
and wondering how you could breathe
while you rest soundly - I will see you then
In the raw nerve of my cognition
I hold my ears while you dive in
I hold my ears and close my eyes
I waste away and you watch, too troubled
by your own distractions to be aware
Your words of animus come
I rest, not a sound may I make this day
You invade what was once peace
Against my back and against my will
You dive in and feel
the sting of eternity's blade
You rape what was once solitude
Amongst the stones I have sat
digging deeper into all that I ever was
Not a molecule unturned
You in your self-pleasing embrace
I have slain, but you remain

"Elysium"

I once watched
from across fields of pavement
as your spark faded
and what once was became
an elegant gasp
in the risen, but forgotten
in my forest of the good,
and tasting your tears
I suffocate and drown
in what you neglect
But I have shaded my eyes
from what you inflict
on yourself, as I begin
to enter my shadow
along forsaken paths
and bask in seclusion once more
Only now I sit, awake
Only now my eyes are open

"Le Odalisque"

Awake to kind words spoken
about a beast who left you broken
Fall asleep with images unshaken
A modern angel who was once taken
Live with a mind which still betrays
Breathe in the one whom life delays
Run from a place where panic ensues
A hug from arms which will soon abuse
A useless soul drifts into tomorrow
To escape a past thick with sorrow
A source of life which I never see
A fool who carries on blissfully
I want to take back the sight
which was once mine
and stab all the vermin
who touched my sunshine
But forward it moves, without me, somehow
What you did then, what I cannot do now
As I melt in the corner, you turn away
with hopes that you'll find me
waiting someday
Though I stifle a scream, you stifle a yawn
and awake to your gift that is now gone

"Patina"

My eyes open in your name
I only see you
Only your voice do I hear
and I know that you listen
When I say you are my everything
I only wish that you could hear me
and help you forget all wrongs
of the past
and I could forget, too
All that's beautiful in this world
is beautiful for you
I need not the moon and the stars
when you have outshined them all

"Absentis"

In the hour of memories and fields of when
With visions in sorrow for you, my friend
The cleansing mist in a raptured hollow
Breathing in pain which I see you swallow
With every tear you cannot hide
to every thorn you lay beside
My hands removed in the silence away
in a verse which the tongue will not say
I dreamed a dream of your placid bliss
Till I tasted the dawn of an empty kiss

"Eremitic"

It is so cold down here
in this land of the muted and unsung
where the children remain hungry
Where the tortured innocent cry, and wish
for their silent, unseen infections to fade
But that horizon can be glimpsed
If they only had the strength
to leave this place
where there are no enemies, only needs
Needs unmet, causes uncured
At least for one more day
Tonight the sun sets
on much more fertile ground
Though it's all just so far away
Here the meek are violated
Their bodies, their souls,
their very essence...
used as playthings by the unevolved
Down here, where there is no justice
Where we all turn our cheeks
and close out mouths
Perhaps it is time for the good
of this world to get even with the bad
but it is just so cold here

"To Await"

Watch me die as I admit defeat
in all your hate
But the wisdom of my yesterday
lays me down
and proves just once
that greener fields are ahead
But will I smile at the collapse of tomorrow?
Each bruise gives me life,
though my ears bleed
from your fountain of energy,
your fountain of lies
I ascend the hills of sanctity
alone and puzzled
No changes I witness for all of your years next
As I was handed words I need not hold,
nor wanted
But take the knife of truth
and press if to your throat
Wash your filthy hands in rules of contention
Pave your fucking road
with the cement of bitterness
and walk until your feet bleed
- still to be found alone
Alone in your shallow valley and blank canvas
My hand will be gone,
as will my vengeful mind
Goodbye to the smug contest of your world

and the rose's paint drips off
the surface of hope
I can smell the insecurity all over you
- fear not
My mouth is shut, but realize
we are the same
Gaze at the sleeping beast
with reckless detachment
It will wake and dismember you
when you forget
Rest well, sweet child,
reality isn't far away tonight
My scars wither and fall as I see again
Keep your eyes closed and yours will go away,
please go away
But it proves just once,
greener fields are ahead

"Noumenon"

In the great distance of our passion
I can feel you in my blood
When I knelt in the fields of Heaven
For every essence of thought you become
I rest in your womb of solemn eternity
Held in your arms, alive within your soul
Serene days awoken upon me
I, a spirit, bestowed unto you
in this restless kingdom of ever
Finding bliss in your memory and
only death in your absence
You were born into my world
with horizons of fantasy told
Still I lay in the midst of solitude
but walk through the sky and yet...
will return to give you my hand again

"Daedalian"

As you lay in your garden of bitter seeds
indulging in tongues of thievery and waste
The night engulfs my gratitude and I rest,
finally, in the thought of blindness to you
Though I have bled your tears again in my
grave of escapes - For now, I breathe,
discovering new flesh within my depravity
Yet I allow my eyes to see beyond your view
...and suffer you will for this, in the rebirth
My darkened path, your pleasant distortion
A thousand flaws spoken in hushed voices
But I hear them - I hear them clearly
Burn, if you must, however, I will be gone
Another lost soul stricken with the scourge
which keeps me falling, yet strangely stable
and your poison I will not possess today -
or ever - for my own is much too strong
The scars of tomorrow
will form without cause
When venomous spirits are never put to rest
All I need is already before me...

"The Corpse of O'Shea"

The corpse of O'Shea, it dwelt by the sea
It killed all the others, but it didn't kill me
He would not stay dead,
that's what they all said
Even though his coffin was made out of lead

Of this they all spoke,
his heart had been broke
By the light of the moon, O'Shea awoke
He made not a sound,
but came out of the ground
They shrieked when
an empty grave had been found

Cold as stone, he was all alone
and the flesh from his hands
had rotted to bone
In the nightly mist, he did insist
to search far and wide for the one he'd kissed

Until it was day, the townspeople say
he killed all the gawkers who got in his way
Their only goal was to bless his soul
and to get O'Shea back into his hole

He would not go wrong,
he would not go right
and he would not go back, without a fight
They all tried bullets and they all tried fire
But the corpse of O'Shea just would not retire

So as months passed, the townspeople cried
and O'Shea still wandered so far and so wide
To this day he still staggers along the shore
This ghoul the townspeople did learn to
ignore

And the corpse of O'Shea
still dwelt by the sea
and he killed all the others, but he didn't kill
me

"The Breach"

Forever is a promise I cannot make
though I will create forever
from nothing for you
I do not want to awake
with you letting this Heaven be cast aside
What you allow to fall away,
some will never see
and I am left to search for answers
Can my mortality become your dream?
At times I sense your eternal wishes clearly
and I try to pass my tarnished soul into
this pristine world - and yet
my gift to you remains in emptiness
Your angelic hunger I cannot appease
When your prayers are so unclear
A requested heart - a given heart
Somehow what is beyond is more tempting

"Rampion"

In my Winter's repose
when I saw her sitting
in the afterglow of rapture
she silently called to me
In an hour's gleaming
I tasted her essence
and a night's dreaming
she came to me
in a sumptuous apology
from my begotten vision
and for one sweet moment
in the bliss of my witness
I breathed her in
and all rivers flowing
slowed in the worship
of our passage
Into her eyes
I fell
and was bound by her answer
From the ecstasy of her kiss
she became my salvation
and my embrace, her home

"The Exile"

You are the face
of the unwanted malcontent
The final ingredient
in the space of undying misery
The shaken hand fallen
from the grasp of malignancy
These are the graces
from worlds of suspension lost
and fractured fingers
which scream your name
Inside your breath I am bound
with untarnished veins which choke
and berate with the fluids of inadequacy
With myself, the failure of decency
the corruption of the vast
I sense your panged want,
your purest answer before the query
So now I stand in the vessel
of premature apology,
hoping the governs of formation
will permit these passings
And I accept the blame
I stand, crimson hand, amongst the fields
of the miraculously guilty

For all the pensive truths
which crawled these lips
in the shade of nearly all rivers
of infectious lies
The sumptuous break, the 'morrow quake
And the protector sees nothing,
yet holds the passage I worship
The skin I admire
Until now I still lay and will die in the fire
When I rupture the core and run dry
of my spirit's last gasp
It bleeds the thick waste
of my begotten vision
And of this, the mass drinks
...and I have nothing left for you
I have nothing left for you

"Femme Desolo"

When my pain shown through
my thinning skin
In the moon of selfish release
where I lay upon chilled hours
When I was engulfed by floods of anguish
in the vengeful name of resolve
On the midnight of my futile passion
and realized surrender,
my weary deception found a way...
And I awake in a new skin
With such callous abandon
...bringing charitable visions
and merciful passage
I was to live once more in your vision
Though I shaded my damaged amity,
the horizon of healing could be heard
from a million miles in your voice
In your being, my torment became
a whispered word
to my deafened ear
...and I am awakened in your smile,
your words,
your emanation
On the day whence I knelt

in the glow of history's ghost
and asked the spirits of sympathy
for a taste of salvation,
it was then that you appeared to me
...and now my eyes have strength
in your name

"In Aeternus Requiescat"

The forgotten days
and the silent screams
of broken days
with untruthful dreams
I sing the song
of painful spells
To right the wrong
in our own Hells
Lead me down
a translucent hollow
Remove my frown
as I watch you follow
In precious never,
we arise then burn
We die forever,
yet never quite learn
With hands in dirt
and rejecting what's real
We ignore hurt
and never will heal
But in the age
of the bittered moon
The passing rage
will fall down soon

127

If we can wait,
our reward will be
a blissful fate
and no misery
A darkened hole
of quiet content
A restless soul
in useless lament
A cozy nest
with comfort deep
and we can rest
in eternal sleep

"Retribution"

I. "The Great Ocean of Malitia"

Though I wade in floods of belief
Your vicious hand was steeped in grief
Misconstrued the pleasure it spoke
in the ashes of bones, your malice broke
Faith is the most sinister disease
on fractured fingers and bloody knees
I hold the tongue which once did speak
and I'll be there when you are weak

II. "The New Flesh"

Savor this consumption from within
as vengeance beholds a fresher skin
it will cover the ground
and smother the sound
of saner thoughts in saner spells
with empty words in deeper wells
it peels when all is scratched and torn
and in this flesh, hatred is born

III. "<u>Wings of Roses and Marrow</u>"

Underneath the fog of rogue malaise
Your blood, my gift of shattered days
I wear your breath with gruesome pride
to sate this thirst which dwelt inside
I drink your tears in selfish lust
to when your teeth have turned to dust
and now you lay on pity's crest
and I will tempt the fate and rest

"Capillary Failure"

I heard the music but once
I discovered my way
within its nestling grasp
and scowled at its moistureless voice
For it was my friend which was my enemy
Towards each perverse undertaking,
for all fallible bodies
which have sobbed in my wake,
I have bled
Bled myself unsavory in the calm breach
of misfortune and blithe
My skin has peeled in the arid silence
of this promise of dust
Gift of needles
I heard the music
and glimpsed the sun ever-so-briefly
and then...forever basked
in the graceless suture,
the harsh blindfold of hair and fingernails
The eternal mute to words
for which the message is sent of disease
the contagion of which you were the carrier
Since the sounds will find no home,
I cease and yield to the damning
and all which subdues me

I saw this all once,
but now I only release
dissimulating antipathy
in my urbane utterance
A weak gasp of vocal immunity sent packaged
in the name of nurturing
The delicious letter bomb of palatial guilt
I'll long to suck you dry in the compass
of threadbare chimeras,
but bring back only the fist of the innocent
Such sickening, vapid layers are placed
on our amatory needs
Waiting for unseen infections to fade
Essences used by the unevolved
Those trivial tidal waves of blackening hunger
where muses of the mind are caught
and muzzled like beasts of savagery
Take the hand of penitence
Feel the insipid strain breach
your unwritten wall
and know that within every wake
I secrete your name
You will never see how I bleed
I heard the music once,
but it is gone

"Ignoratio Elenchi"

Soft, fleshy peelings made of tin falling,
devoid of putrefying grace,
into cylinders of slick, oily rivers
with blackened testimonials
gestating and boiling
in undercurrents blanketed beneath
heavy, swollen sutures
Itching, breaking, weeping seams
unfolding and exposing
Pulsating, penetrating muscles
within the flowing contagion
Tightened orifices gushing,
molten praise and soiling
smooth, sticky clearings
of corrupted throats eating
through layers of Styrofoam nail,
liquefying into lakes of pure in vitro
Particle board urethras
sprout nails under shade
of cancer showers from
puncturing tempura skin grafts
shredded in glycerin teeth
Burning fumes of napalm toothpaste
and sweet, syrupy bleedings
of insulin streaming
from the breach in my Plexiglas lungs...

"King of Masks"

There's a stain on my floor
from the day I died of grief
For all I once was, melting away again
and he winter speaks this agony in fallen gods
and I awoke once again
in the aftermath of vision
Its lying tongue a thousand years removed
Inviting the soul, I scratch until bruised
But the wounded remains silent
in our tormented ocean
Empathy beneath my nails
I remain silent amongst exquisite sheep
Resting to expend this plague of you
My flesh paler, to smother all blame
the simplistic wonder
of unknowing intervals when...
Though I swallow your corrosive serum
Once I drowned in your distance
And wasted away in slavery's embrace
Tasted the angst of your impending dusk
I see you dance in the waves
of remorseless skin
When the noose tightens,
your hand to dust becomes
Savor the taste of the weeping pearls
and sands of bruises

My reflection laughs for what I've become
and drowns in a sea of crooked will
and suffocates on wasted breath
Domestic freaks my acquaintance
There's still a stain on my flesh
From the day I tasted
the sleep of nothingness
And the voices, though they may never come

"God from the Machine"

I.

So I was.   So I am.
The grey blotch of existence came upon me
like the muddled jabberings of a lunatic
buried away in the back
of some abandoned place,
never to be embraced by the remainder
of the populace
A missing grief, an absent plea
from this weakening
undergone, discloses tales
of ill manners and vessels
of the lamented masses
And so my screams went unheard as well,
just as they had begun so early
...and stung so deeply
With this falling of the night I finally bestow
unto others the knowledge
that I had always been without grasp
My hands clutched pointlessly
at the rope which controlled
the background scenery I walk before
to this very day
after so many years of what
has amounted to so little

...and I know now that it was not I
who formed any rational thought
It was not I who was ever in control
In this, there are less glass shards from father
to hold you safe in this dwelling of instability
Like the trees who watch helplessly
as their beautiful leaves turn,
fall, and crumble
...only to begin again
in the passing of months
Though my leaves have never grown again
So you ask about the time
when they clutched the tip of every twig
back in my early years
and how I wish I could tell you
about how effortlessly they rustled
in the wind
...and with such wonder
I wish I could, but it began so early
that I can hardly recall any of it
without something poisoning the well
Yet I smiled, time and again,
thinking to myself,
"So at peace with the storm you've gifted me.
Though with you gone, the storm has
departed."

II.

I rolled and grumbled softly
...and spoke quietly to myself words
Words that I now caressed closely to,
like an infant against its mother's
silken, warm skin
They nourished me as such, as well
I wrapped my hand tightly around the wet,
rusted chain that hung ominously
in the center
of the unholy cell
This tongue is damned and the hail
of the great passage is
preventing you from breathing
upon your lusting table
Entreated for the laurel
to shed such attirement
and propel my undying scorn
within the consecrated aperture
But wishes wither, much like our whole
as we are eaten away at from within by beasts
of disease and age, never knowing full well
that we are not in control
What we want, we will not get
They are watching
They are playing with us
We are slaves to them, just as
we perceive them
to be slaves to us

They laugh as we bleed, feed as we suffer
This was all so clear to me now
as their gnawing fluid dripped down
on me from high above
I simply wanted my eyes to be spared
They were not.   So be it
In the meantime, I smiled
and thought to myself,
"So at peace with the storm you've gifted me.
Though with you gone, the storm has
departed."

"Modus Operandi"

Here is my sweetened loneliness
The immortal and blessed unrest
Longing of the incarnate sting
of the bead of sweat
in the ailing eye
Benevolent spoonfuls
of cream and discontent
Blissful and punctured lay
the unspoken and destitute
Here lays I
In the sardonic vice
of withering means,
between almighty contagion
and incredible shapes,
crestfallen with the offense
of gratuitous pangs
Cyclical dreams of infected colors,
ulterior wonders
That childlike deception
and pasteurized fingerprints
Still, we plea to the sterile
and certified
A mind which reigns
in the withholding of lunacy
Those orgiastic treats which never return,
vanishing into the horizon of continence

Off they slip beyond the tracks of blame
The sired, disgraced,
which collapse in my name
and cry out for the strain
to release the disdain
Blackened atrocities
in their gelatinous disfigurement
which furnish my inner regions
Such decorations need not make
their presence known quite so often
Requests unanswered
Undesirables come freely
and in plentiful numbers
When I wake, I will sing of purity painted
in hideous tones and a misplaced Eden
I will walk the mile of pathos
which rip at my greater senses,
horrible senses
I taste not of annihilated beauty,
but of concentrated stoicism
Though in ways of palindromic resistance,
I see this thirst extinguishing
upon the very stone
from whence it was fertilized
The westborn sun also rises
in the yesterday cult of my intrusive palate
I soon shall become the noon of temperance
Temperance
I wish only to taste your thick nectar,
pleasant temperance

Though turned away blindly
by the mountains of inability,
I rise once more
in the torrents of astringence
Though gently I approached,
confrontation is severe
in my essential balance
of poisonous roads
I see what is unstable in our theories
of the secure and peaceful
I wonder quietly,
like minor scrapes and insect bites,
why we choose to bathe
in the waterfalls of the callow
Oblivious vision and unwitting ears
Bound hands and muted feet
Still I creep into your jagged lament
in the silken acrylic blade
of your mistrustful pleasantries
I walk here for the scent of decaying claws
with dirty spirits that have rewritten the book
and dance heavy with forsaken drones
Forever glancing in
the direction of definition,
which I see with blurred eyesight
and misshapen speak
I will trade in my pride for the ill-gotten dose
of recycled sense and the cold lip
of stalled melanoma fusion
which bleeds the tree

and pins down my sunken want,
my questionable ethics
and releases only those that lurk
...lurk underneath my adhesive,
stone-meshed remedies
I will cry no more for all I once was
and embrace the rankled image
which floats just
on the upside of the dripping essence
of melting reflection
and the malfeasant birth
I look kindly upon the fetus
who withdraws from the disarray,
but wakes once again to braver things
in the sequential brightness
...and shutter when proposed of the strength
of face who falls with his own ego
Let that not be me, I pray
...though not to a myth, but to a dream

"Servile Manifest"

Soon to be taken by a rest of the damaged,
the vehement taste of our insane deceit
My entwining cage quivers and aches,
honoring desperate you
Pleasantly infected by delicious menace

Your beckons unheard this eve
...though the morn has promise
In this world of stolen feelings
and synthetic passions
For this eve, memories carry knives
whispering our name
I clinch my eyes on transparent lids

The past sun found us laughing
with careless abandon
I am asleep in purple suns
with torturous pride
but these stars drop handfuls
of contentment and indifference
The insects of society
as they claw at my release

When I climb under protection
in a cloud of withdrawal
(with your frozen grin,
with your emoting pills)

is the time when you should find your sky
filled with concern
Yet I wrap myself in your precious animus

For I have bled the truth
and swallowed the furor...
engulfed my all
in your insecurity...
and laid down in the shadow
of violators passing through
In my fallen care,
in my circle heart

In this final hour,
I wait for the sweet call of the just
The ground whispers complacently
in the aftermath song
But it is not listening
Never have I felt secure in its hand

As we leap into the graves of conformity
A deep breath which destroys
my precious wonder
Awakening such alive intensity of the dead
I, a leaf in your forest as it burns

Fade away with your ill-gotten gains
Stop and ponder
...to wait for decay or burn myself
Your selfish accomplishments

of disguised avarice
With every path I've descended
in search of your melancholy

Revel in your poisonous spirit and breathe
I defend my right to be alert
and no longer the child
Breathe in the madness of your logic
Breathe it in and suffocate...and live not

Turning my head to
a gathering of passive beasts
Lost again, when denial can be drank
from overflowing heavens
and the guilty inherit the soil
...we drift downward
Never dreaming of a day
when they will discover weakness
and it will be our turn
And it will be our turn

It is then that my hand
will find the strength once
to twist the knife
of repression and release my grin
I realize now the definition of nothing, awake
What's right and wrong
is sitting just to the left of me
In this final hour,
I dare not speak their name...

"Minde Perceptum"

What guilty hands have I...
With morose, dwindling nerves
and they still work - make no mistake
Time is a pill which dissolves in violence
Not easily forgotten - my bleeding sympathy
Destroyed in the valley of the confused
Wrong for being what I am, what I desire
Though I walk through your ignorance
and enjoy the view
Seems like salvation has failed once more
in the shattered vessel of cruel repose
and diligent squander
Pick up the pieces, hold them in your jealousy
Dine upon your kin, the feast of bones
The lie that helps you sleep at night
A bitter moon held dear again
Breached solace while peace wastes away
Wipe that dependence off of your face
The obvious soil you dare not pass
The soft, pink mundane razorwire
Your patterns crumbling
in your careful denial
While your urgent mind sleeps
in abscessed faces
in the distance of complacency
Exquisite bile with the taste
of our insane deceit

Pleasantly infected by delirious menace
In the world of stolen feelings
and synthetic passions
In vitro dreams and companion by syringe
Begging of my throat to close on irrelevance
A chateau of indulgent affect,
my skin wish infringement
begets the sour twilight
and acid-eroded, sleepless eyes
Happiness is a serum
you will never drink down
and love is but penetration, invasion,
humiliation...no more
My callous reckoning a lie said in angst
of a passing necrosis
Sinking into your discolored rapture,
your draining stare
Your ungiving smile
contaminates my absence
Engulf my all in your salivating insecurity
The ground whispers the aftermath hymn
But there are no ears to catch it
As we leap into the graves of conformity
and drown in menstruating gulfs
Awaking such alive intensity
of the erect begone
Your selfish accomplishments
of disguised want
With those infected offerings I taste the
sweetness of breath,

my harsh abundance
Mirthless spirits in the hours of trite,
clutch of the frozen undying
This element of perception in my haunted
name, the absurd awakening
But, oh, what guilty hands have I...

"Scientia Sexualis"

Awakened the absorption to salve the burn
in the color of unfavorable penetration
and the beast comes out
still dead in your lap, I'll be
where there is no release
but passioned leers and razorwire memories
The agonized wait within the wretched's state
where the foul advance
and the immaculate wait

Time is wasting in aluminum friction
Washed off the teeth and danced
The pills of relics, centurion catastrophe
Toes broken and shamed, cracked...
leaking the latex immunity
where there is still no release
but techno-colored forgiveness

Blessed with sterility
The ethical salutation, the forgotten pulse
Dead weight upending the structure
The gloriously capsized
The colonoscopy of promises
where there is still no release
The slaves of a proverbial fork
in severed tendons

Swallowing impurity in each withdrawal
of stiffening disconcern
seamlessly blends with blissful disregard
The nymphatic begets the bisected matriarch
in all absent punctures
which dig in, though never lacerate
Pierce but not rupture, flow forth nicht
and there will never be respite

"Maeror Meror"

The love I feel for you must vanish
with the shapes of time passing
I can feel it undoing us both
I had grieved my losses until
I had held you close
in my dream,
but soon comes the morn
And with daybreak did I lose you
I lost with you
the shattering of unconsciousness
And though I would bleed
for you in beautiful sorrow,
I know I have not the power
to raise the ghost of never
Though I have tried
With every tear
which scratched its way
down my burning cheek
I have tried
for it is my birth
which walked hand-in-hand
with unending failure
I suffer in your name
as you do in mine
The gravity of teeth crushing
what could have been eternity

"Crimson"

All around me in subdued silence
Echoing throughout
and forever besieged
by your absence,
a prisoner in a tomb of tranquility
Solitude is my name
Grief is my being
Giving forth a sensation
of vitality
Descending upon a thrust
of distress
in a land of graceless images
stimulating an impaired existence
into unwanted growth
Rain becoming needles
Life flowing from a current
adapting to the moisture
the dank air defiling you
Each breath an eclipse
tasting the spirit
of what is now gone
Suffer before departure
Wrath dissolving your purest instinct
Blown away like ashes
in your spell
Reflecting on a wandering chill
An angel bearing bloodied treasures

Forever besieged
by your presence
Becoming a servant to the waves
All around my in subdued silence,
if solely in my mind

"Funereal Song"

Lurid chapters within my route
Finding me waiting
with stained passions
and broken visions
of a time less seen
Upon the dusk,
an entwining stands
before you in a cavity
of distorted seasons
A birth of purity
in a state of disease
in the cry of
anguish's child
Pierced and impaired
by your clarity
A shaping clutches your doubt
Thrusts you into
familiar solitude
Taken into my embrace
remolded into a presence
Sliced open by your affection
corrupted by your sympathy
Drag me out of the marsh
Bury me in the soil
of your judgement
Remove yourself from
the frigidity of my all

and I feel your rage
pour down onto my shoulders
decaying and establishing
an enemy of substance
where the grass grows red
sleeping high in the trees
watching down upon you,
mouth forever closed,
basking in the sound
of patience
and evermore possessing
an escape damp with torment

"To Kate"

I feel as though it's time I speak
in this time of futures bleak
a time when grays have become black
when those I love will not come back

Perhaps I only know your word
Perhaps your voice I've never heard
and so I've never felt your touch
I will not renounce a soul as such

We tread this evil ground will dwell
You emerge a sharer of my Hell
In time, I've felt my wanting grow
to bask in the light of your glow

In this shadow of wanton lies
I behold a horizon within your eyes
How profound to your ear my plea?
How long I continue solemnly...

I beseeched of you to with me walk
Forever devout of which I talk
Alas, I am cursed by the hand of fate
I'm to be forgotten by my dearest Kate

"Human Benign"

Lay me down in the aftermath
of your perverse undertakings
in the barren mental plains
with so little ground gained
shedding gallons
of efforting fluids
only to awake
still amongst the negatives

"Et Mentis"

I no longer fear
that which leaves me stolid and painless
For it was not without warning
No one listened
Only complained
Deeply I dove
into the petrified flesh
of victimized drones,
unaware of the ever-ringing effects
of their selfish and ignorant ways
I took your poisoned hand
and allowed you to make me the fool
when the carnivorous seconds
of the ages
violate our movement,
the fallen sculpture
of the masses
will rise again
But these inhabitants
do not smile
No blood
No stone
The aberrations will come
and cry not
as they cut off the lips
which form a grin
Long lingering

in the seed of corruption
watching you embrace devils
Taken away into the moist grasp
of the upright, walking sods
of deprogrammed insects
I come from the ocean
where I cannot speak or breathe
A festering chemical
which washes ashore
and clings to molded rocks
in an attempt to breed with nature
and with I, standing
in the face of accusations
A vessel for such acid
Loneliness in the name of greed
and standing to become infected
by the silent and the faceless

"Calamitas"

I sleep in pain of a poisoned rain
At night I hear your song
I scream your name, a beast to tame
and how it turned out wrong

I wanted to be your deep blue sea
instead I became your bane
My window black and starting to crack
as a king of the insane

Your call unheard, my life absurd
You need more than my love
A soul of fear which wants you near
You look down from above

You are nowhere, I want to be there
To me, you are a wave
A sharpened knife which gives me life
For all which you have gave...

...and then took away, and since that day
I have not been the same
It's far too late to hold such hate
for what we then became

We had it all, began to fall
and did not try to hold on

It tore apart and in my heart
I know it is now gone

Raw and rare, a breath of air
Which did not last too long
A perfect kiss, our united bliss
Which somehow all went wrong...

"Betrothal"

The long, narrow path
which finds me stricken
An unending wrath may forever thicken
in the river of being, this hallowed view
My eyes are seeing a clearer you
The era of hurt, my greatest fear
My hands in the dirt, your voice I hear
and for all your words, for near and far
In each passing year I've searched for my star
Though I may be blind to the given sign
I know what I seek will always be mine
Holding it near, I will not let go
and each precious tear, I will let you know
On shadowy nights
when I am lost somewhere
Through wrongs and rights, you are still there
Watching and waiting for me to awake
and for all my sadness to finally break
When at last I see your patience has grown
All you mean to me will then be known

"Salvus"

I could try to forget you
in my hollow tomorrow
I could find myself waiting
in a sullen wish
For the one thing I've needed
in the strength of infinity
I've found in your senses
in the hold of this day
My reason to be
and open my eyes
Into the embrace of ethereal you
In the years of contempt
where I questioned the sounds
You remained
Even when my deafened ears
heard no more songs
and my mind a beacon
of torture and angst
You remained
a promise of unweathered nights
In my mind you stayed safe
In the corners of dignity
and in the shade of perception
You stayed
in my still-wounded heart
Your face
Always resting
Always knowing

"Satis"

In the cusp of the river of infamy
lies this circle of ire inside of me
from the black seas of agony pure
in the selfish strain without any cure
The icy chill of humanity's whole
Hence stands a being without any soul
In the name of the pill, there sees your voice
Entities of unrest which remove your choice
When demons rest in utter displease
and reason is gone in the rustling trees
Through each forest we rise
in search of a sound
with an eye for all
the deception we've found
Step through conceit, kneel on the path
Stand in my way and suffer my wrath
The sparrows of fate await your return
so the eyes of the dead can watch you burn
and hypocrisy can claim yet another child
when the soft of our flesh is again defiled
who will praise the one who stands and falls
and read all their writing on asylum walls
I am here with no face for you all to see
just this circle of ire that's inside of me
And when someday you know of this,
your mistake
You will not be absolved
when I watch you break

"Affinité"

Unto the depths
of whence my love has gone
Into the horizon
my love rests upon
Beyond the mountains and fields
my love hath crossed
Above all the sorrow
my love hath lost
Passed many a soul
my love found untrue
But below the Heavens
where my love found you

'Tis where my love
came drifting down
Into my eyes
and a life unsound
No cries of my love
now go unheard
A chill of comfort
befalls each word
or the very air
breathed in by my love
How may I touch
thy hand from above?

"Burgundy"

As you sit so close
our touch only brief
A tiny little dose
to stifle my grief
If only you saw
what I feel inside
That day may you rue
for I no longer hide
Three times around
perhaps maybe four
My soul I have found
but still I ignore
Your spirit I feel
Your essence I hold
Past wounds will not heal
but come back ten fold
In my mind you are kept
your face I can see
Every night I have slept
with you watching me
An obtuse love
a vision of pain
Below or above
Alone I remain
Your affection's not mine
as you walk away
I slip from the line
to face another day

"Mia"

If the swallows of evil
consume my dawn
a part of you
I can never touch
The warmth of your love
falling from my stance
and the shadow of content
I will never
part ways with your eyes
and I linger
with words shielding me
from all that chains me
Finding my passion
within your grasp only
Every tear which escapes me
is in your name
Each step taken
will be by your side
With me wear no mask
sooner shade the sun

"Limbs of Ash"

I die a thousand deaths
in the hollow of your voice
when the forest gives way
as I furious wipe
at your lips
unable to remove the stain
forever tarnishing
and slashing the air
and mutilating us all
crushing below our feet
like the leaves
of an Autumn solstice
and a dark wind blows
when I feel myself draining
My fluids being used
as the ink of the spectres
and I hear their laughter always
Furious laughter
The penalty of a soul without doubt
Blissfully unaware of the agony
you've given birth to
a misery with my name

"Despoil"

To see inside
to the darkest core
Your eyes, they swell,
and then see no more
The burning wings
on the fall from stability
The angel, she sings,
but sings in hostility

"Encomium"

My heart is an ocean
in which you swim,
an eternal passage of beauty
and limitless wonder, unreachable
The space between us,
a subconscious cruelty
The wind wonders
and whispers to me -
messages of awe,
passages I listen to intently,
all from the mouth of you
When I can hear no longer
I will still listen
My compassion endless for you
though I will not resolve your pain
in the words of my subconscious
In this, my undying promise
need not be clearer
in spirit, if not in flesh
Of lives and of dreams
you call to me
A threshold never
to be crossed
A torturous feat
unknown to man
You have become
my emotion's holder
and I bleed with you

while standing in the sunshine
of your possession
and slipping, so swiftly
into the valley of echoes
where angels dare not
show their faces
Where memories dance
in hollow fortresses
and my hand grasps empty space
and the cold gusts of Autumn
cry for the warmth
of your aura
Cherished, though not deserved
I am humbled in your presence
A life unfulfilled
without your touch

"Stolid"

This thorn in my side
the humid core lifting
mingling with the ghosts
of hatred,
Clutching the sheets tightly,
body pressed down, deep
A struggle of wills and unrest
with my enemy, sleep
My hands, wet
The enigma of my neck and spine
And such grim illusions
upon the eve of moving forward
into the twinges of grief
It swells upon motion
like it senses I am awake
The drift is deceitful
for my soul's sake
Clutching the sheets tightly
body pressed down, deep
A struggle of wills and unrest
with my enemy, sleep

"The Cessation"

The red moons shine down
beyond the graying hills
as I wait for the tide
with the soil around my knees
and speaking to the silent voices
while you feast on the
givings of agony
and I fall from grace in your name
and it echoes across the sea
as I rest in slumbered remorse
and my walls grow larger
as you reach into my burning heart
You touch with bloody fingers
and we shed our skin
and when flesh becomes bone
and the greening flowers sway
The ocean calls our name
The moonlight shines down
and impurity I can smell
all over your falling skin
laughing at our keeper
and committing your first sin
We are pleasantly blinded
across this sacred land
and now falls a blackened rain

"Revenant"

They fall with the rain tonight
crawling through my head
consuming a sadness
and releasing a blistering coldness
I close my eyes
as they come through the trees
with regret walking behind me
and my blue hands closing
to a numbing unrest
and the spectres of guilt
from the surface, from the deep
reflect for empty years
in a dying breath
which dries your tears
In a dawnless night
My fingers still run
through your hair
Though I open my eyes
as they come through the trees
to take you away
and I fall with the rain tonight

"Black Blood"

Deep in the realms
of your liar's tongue
I watch it split
and stand in the stream
of the bile of its deceit
Your captivating face
masks a demon's soul
and I was pushed
aside once more
as you crawled
from your whole
and a million shapes
your voice
your corrosive saliva
burns the surface
eating through layers
and causing growths
and you became
the greatest era
of disease
and I became tainted
in your presence
and with you
in my vision
my eyes go black

"Quis Separabit"

I.

Me, I am a thing of nature
Me, I am and have been displaced
Me, I have no real identity
Me, I once was something great

II.

Once upon a time we were all a miracle
Once upon a time we were all in soil
Once upon a time I could say you've hurt me
Once upon a time I could say I am sorry

III.

In time you'll see that you're not damaged
In time, perhaps, I'll become more clear
In time I'll find that I am wanted
In time you'll know that I'm still here

"One"

From the rain that falls
from the blackened sun
In the sorrow of it all,
I am one
When I look deep into
the dried up sea
Am empty space
my heart used to be
I find sweet regret
to be my friend
My razorblade smile
till the very end
What soul have I
left to give you?
How many painful days
left to live through?
My sadness, my madness
You swallow every drop of me
You stand by my side
in this pleasant misery
With every twinge
of remorse I may feel
Under a blanket of dispirit,
You make me real
Alive in your presence
each absence I die
Your precious image heals

the wound that is I
Years ahead, when all
is said and done
In the fortune of now,
we are one

"Inertia"

If I could trust my own reflection
The crack which breaks the dam
If I could kill you with discretion
I might find out who I am

"Saints and Bastards"

With the joyfully embraced
and the irritable forgotten
In the visage of expiry
laying pierced
in existence's anarchy
with the neglection of your name
in the convenience of sorrow
You grasp of the dissipated exertion
giving it titles
and granting it forms
licking the remaining stain
of a stigma called Fate

"Espirit de corps"

In the random undertaking
not the deed of miscreants
an acceptance given
in vanity
in a chance to let destiny rest
Leave it to repose
and regenerate
for all the new ages
in the want of more serendipity
than Karma's hands
could ever weave
Allow the glass seraphic mask
to fall
and smash into tiny splinters
of our own ignorance
and simplicity
in the parable of evolution
and move backwards
Under seventy-two
inches of dirt
we all become saints
and only bastards breathe

"Perverta Non Grata"

You were given
a dehydrated rebirth
suffocating on wasted will
in the refuge of a palindrome
Of a hollow tree
with more fear and less comfort
walking the streets
of profane wrath
and sleeping in the trust
of failing defects
Searching the clay
of enigmatic rivers
Picking the wounds
and tasting the stigma of conceit
and the pavement of defeat
Pulling, hard, until
the muscle rips
in the pleasured tremors

Benign traces nil explained
Societal faces leave you drained
Absolute is the nerve
in every bruise,
every doubt which follows you
The slaves will rise
with open mouths
to have their say
To break the skin
To rape the heart
and fucking fade away

"Plastic Theol"

Salvation displays
in ashes wrung
in lawns ablaze
when captors sung
in smiles bound
your passive trap
my sacred ground
in fortune's map
emotional theft
the dank dissention
a sound bereft
the heart's invention
Dishonest need
your bravest sin
A selfish deed
alike your kin
An angelic wraith
with scorn belief
The loss of faith
The birth of grief
Take my place
my field of dust
and hold your face
in pleasant rust

"The Qui of Mephitic Unrest"

This calm perception
of faultless being,
a sentient apathy in erratic resolve
A sound which is written
upon suspicion's shoulder
beneath heavy courses
of irreverent allure
A voice found bound
by the frigidity of belief
That caustic little puncture
following forced consumption
of motionless solidity,
languishing within every recess
of our own disdain
It is gone, the ache of anxiety,
a beautiful spasm bestowing ecstatic floods
of effusive remission, of my urgency,
you bring death on your lips
And the pressing prominence reappears,
calling deafening names
and manifesting appalling portraits unseen
in their inestimable detest
And all eventual demands come
piercing the void,
wretching and pulling a cursory edge
across supple exteriors
The age of defile

The breach of the flawless
It exudes immodest solutions
from its inner walls, shedding,
cleansing the feculent fleece,
only to grow another
...and steal away into servile fragments,
awaiting fresh tribulation
and peculiar regret
Though extravagant sediment dreams
of naive pleasure
in sublime offerings,
the invention of endurance,
he stares,
furiously wiping at the stigma
which eternally defects
the visage of his reason
A gesture of naked palms,
breeding new oceans
of the deafeningly mute,
all becoming one
in an undertow
of perfect calm
A calm perception
of faultless being
This tyrannical failure
of the blistering profane,
uttering infections
and singing penetration
The seedlings of insignia
and her leprous shavings,

burning with choking retinas
...still awaiting, once again
the caustic little puncture

"Emaciate"

Coming to the end
of all which was endured
The current of you
a worthless skin
in passioned voices
which make no sound
and remaining awake
in absence of a face
with your glutinous resolve
adhering to my fingers
seeing only the impurities
of disquiet
and insignificant eloquence
upon subversive shelter
Time and again
I have risen once more
and screaming in silence
The ecstasy of your deceit
weeps craven pretension
with shades of simple deficiency
and I will no longer watch
as the demons defile you
knowing you allowed them
and scratch my eyes

until I am blind
Meaningful words
will now fade
Hearing only the hatred
which is in your song

"The Quiet Demise"

Unable to recall
a time of greater peace
as I am relieved of my flesh
and they feed upon me
feeling their claws digging in
with a smile which never leaves me
in a bitter taste of bile
with all the acid in my wake
and gestating within
becoming something
less than human
and savoring every fold
of my sullen skin they peel
and they pick off the dead
and I cried not
for my anguished soul
as it dissolved below me
in the retreat
of a rotated spine
and the searing delight
of an empty cavity
and they become nourished,
thirsts quenched
by my poisoned well

"The Cusp of Odium"

The nest of triviality
shown through thinning layers
and tiresome become the wretches
of insolent abandon
in the vengeful name of resolve
On the midnight
of my futile passion
and kerosene surrender
Feet grinding the poverty
of in vitro drenched cliffs
Thick about me without escape,
an inefficient refuge
and charitable dehydration
of your illicit rebirth
You became this whorish amity
A spontaneous combustion
of silken skin pictures
of lithesome dreams
and savory carbonation
The heart failure embrace
A pathetic little merciful hemorrhage
with a name
Now all but a whisper
to a deafened ear
A parasitic emanation
from my shaded disinterest

A million miles in your voice
could be heard from a glass cage
The things you wouldn't dream to defend
A callous on the tongue of liberation
You live in my fractured eyes
The nefarious horizon
of the septic baptism
and your cheerful laceration I lick clean
Something you cannot comprehend

"The Fall"

Take my hand and we will walk off into that
cellophane rainforest of the troubled concrete
shell of particle moments and digital solitude.
Put your trust in my solid white landscapes
and you'll forever bask in the meaning of the
romantic Rogaine which speaks the verbal
aneurysm of your pleasantries.   Filled with
disappointment when I see the look of
mistrust written across your face in the inks
of the slaughtered, even though I have given
you the leather tumor of friendship as I
pushed the machete of lies deep into your
spine and watched the beautiful shock spill
out.   I tried to prevent it from stinging, but
you moved too soon.   I'll be certain to pull
your head up quickly before you can drown in
the kerosene which has dripped down the lips
of the gorgeous parasites and forms
wonderful pools of corrosion.   Fear not.   I
will lift you.   I will end your misery even if it
means I have to triple it first.   Whereas once
you were lost, now you are...lost, still.   Little
orgasmic wretch, you are.   An ejaculate fool
of the human monarchy who never once
looks down to see whom you've stepped in.
I removed my own gallbladder today, just to

see how long I could survive without silver, swollen eccentricities.   I did it all with your assistance.   Your mystical failure and your acidic nurturing.   There should be no doubt in you as long as you are under my alkaline tutelage.

No need to worry as your skin becomes cancerous and your feet sink deeply into the starving hypocritical ground beneath you. It's expected.   It's as normal as the paste which seals your eyes closed like a fungus that is only birthed whence you speak my name aloud.   I am the eternity.   Taste me. Feed off the nauseous brine of your egotistical polyester and your subconscious delusion. Your tongue is that antibacterial enigma which drifts like flakes of dried, dead peelings and lines my cherry cheesecake insulation with the embryonic fluid of desperation dust.
You are uncarved vinyl.   You are the ruptured vessel that stifles airflow.   Feed off me still.   Drink down this teething seed and then lick yourself clean in my name.   Fulfill the cardiac incision in my name.   Open that ribcage and let in the softness of jealous innocence.   Let it rape and molest your blind burial, for I am your lead balloon.   I am struggle.   I am sickle-cell anemia for the elitist and prosecuted.   You can ride this

verbal snack until the vacant nobodies beg
you to come down.   Come down and ingest
the gristle of perfection.   I could wipe your
mouth now, but I'd just as soon get a tan.
Tan and recover.   Recover and rust.   Clean
off and haunt cancer again until I can't
breathe.   But it's out of my hands.   And you
will see all and choke on me.   Exit.   I'll
make sure you choke.

"An Atrophy Befalls Us"

...and comes the sainted,
the blameless insignia
which extends the atrophied hand
only in fringe
only in fringe
and brings a murrain
in her selfish smile
with festering malignancy
behind her deteriorating eyes
The aberration she holds
between the chasm
of an absent anima
languishing long in the confines
in the hollow of her verve
in the capacious vacancy
of all that she is
That empty promise
in words of fallacy
so filled with animus
which blinds her
it blinds her
to all that could save her

"Regina"

Every breath
draws her further away
inspiring one to cease
with life withering
below me in shards
of graying vivacity
where there was once green
which illuminated
the fields at night
in the coils of
my sweetest downfall
which now slip from my hands
and gift me only disease
in the aftermath of solitude
without her glow
Grasping not her hand
but only my dreams
that one day she will awake
in the calm morning
and be warmed
by the memory
and she will follow
the lights home

"Virago"

To bring you back
every last drop
and cries unheard
when lies from the saints come
and the demons rising
in my unconscious state
seeking your voice
as my soul, it departs
in the embrace
of the strongest emotion
and the gate closes behind me
in the tears of
an immortal cringing
with you finding yourself
within my pace
and damning your resistance
while drinking deep
the poisoned karma
and you watch as I
haunt the loneliest place
and filling the emptiest chair
for the sleep of always
In the empty well of spirits
To bring you back,
every last drop,
returning to me all that I was
before the fall

INDEX

www.ingramcontent.com/pod-product-compliance
Lightning Source LLC
Chambersburg PA
CBHW071429090426
42737CB00011B/1605